A Small Steadying Sail of Love

Poems, Meditations and Photographs

Nancy Gibbs Richard

Nancy Gibbs Richard

Angela Center Press

First Edition

Angela Center Press, 535 Angela Drive, Santa Rosa, CA 95403
www.angelacenterpress.org
707.525.8578

Book and cover design by Bruce Conway,
Illumina Book Design, Friday Harbor WA 98250
www.illuminapublishing.com

Printed in the U.S.A. on recycled paper

Library of Congress Control Number: 2007933991

$16.00

ISBN 0-9729343-4-0
ISBN 978-0-9729343-4-3

For my husband Charles
who long has been
a steadying sail of love
in my life.

I write in praise
of sacred mystery
and joys
that catch us by surprise,
love's unexpected sweetness,
and all that brings us
fully alive.

There is evidence
threaded throughout my life story
that I have been strengthened
and guided at every turning.
Now is the time to trust
that this will continue to be true.

I cannot save the world
or heal another person's hurts,
but I can offer
one small act of kindness
at a time.

Surrendering our wanting
to a bigger truth
opens us to a bigger life.
Drop down
into that deeper knowing,
and trust that you
will be guided in a way
that is good for you to go.

On seas of grief
my boat and I
weather storms
of terrible sorrow
with a small
steadying sail of love.

How often do we refuse
the gifts that are given,
rejecting human love
because of its imperfections?
"Not what I want or need,"
we say, pulling our loneliness
in closer around us
as if to comfort ourselves
with an afghan of righteous
indignation.

O God, rock me
in the arms of the universe,
hold me
in the heart of healing,
sing me songs
of the sacred mysteries,
and I will be comforted
in my sorrow
and strengthened
in the fearful places
of my life.

A Prayer for My Birthday

May I live fully each moment I am given,
delighting in life,
not wasting anything on worry.
May I recognize the blessings
of the people I love
and of those who challenge me to grow.
May I live a life of joy, peace and gratitude,
trusting that my steps will be guided,
my heart filled, my spirits lifted,
no matter where I am
or what my circumstances may be.
May this be so.

The Logistics of Leaving

a house that I love—
a house filled with light
and views of the water,
Lopez Island, Cattle Point,
seal covered rocks,
bald eagles in flight,
a great blue heron fishing—
require not only the usual
practical planning,
hard letting go of much
and packing up of the rest,
but also a new mapping
of my heart's terrain.

From ponds and creeks
to inland seas and ocean beaches,
my love of light on water
is like laughter—
it goes with me everywhere.

The Landscape of Loss

Walking again
in the landscape of loss,
it is hard to get my bearings.
I have walked this way
many times before,
but the paths have changed
and so have the losses
that bring me here.
Far easier to comfort another
than to give voice to my own grief,
but it is in this terrain
that I will find my tears.

In memory of Nikki Palecek

God is

in the absence
and the presence,

in the joy
and the sorrow,

in the pain
and the healing,

in the waiting
and the journey,

in the darkness
and the light.

Soul becoming
more luminous,
heart more
transparent to God—
not waiting,
may I learn
to live this way now.

In memory of Guy Littman

What words can speak
of the deepest sorrow?
Where lies comfort
for the despairing heart?
O God, be with me
in the darkest places—
hold the promise
of the Light.

Gathering together with the Spirit
to allow space for my sorrow,
to take time for my tears—
this is just what I need now—
Meeting for Worship for Weeping.

What keeps me apart
from the heart of God?
Why do I pull back
from that healing,
holy touch?
My life is held
with tenderness,
regardless
of what I believe
or think I know.
How difficult it is
to relinquish
the illusion of control
and entrust my life
to the Holy One
who unfolds
my path before me,
as I walk it, step by step.

With prayers
for peace in my heart
and a quiet mind,
I enter stillness
where Presence
is palpable
and listen for sounds
of that holy touch.

December

As the days darken down
in this year's ending,
what in me awaits
healing transformation,
what new life
is preparing to be born?

I need to clear out
the closets of my soul
to make room
for the timeless,
the unexpected,
the new.

Radical Acceptance

Of who you are,
the life you live,
the choices you make—
I cannot pick up
your consequences
or accept misplaced blame,
but I will bless you
on your way
and trust that you are held
in God's love and mercy.
This is the path of peace for me.

This also is true:
it may be possible
to meet
in a place of tenderness
with a person
whose troubles trouble you.

Can You Hear Me?

We are separated by the wild river
of all that is unspoken.
With this small rock
I throw the first line across.
Tie it securely.
Let the building of the bridge begin.

There is a God-space between us
that holds a truth
larger than any of our own.
It is a challenge to be open
to that possibility,
to trust the Great Mystery
of the in-between-place
that can move us towards
forgiveness, reconciliation, home.

O God,
stitch up my heart
with golden thread.
May a new strength grow
in the broken places.
Give me the courage
to feel the pain of betrayal
and the compassion to let it go.
Teach me to forgive myself
as I struggle to forgive others.
And where there are no answers,
may the questions become a prayer.

We invite God
into our conversation,
make room in our hearts
for wholeness,
surrender our need to be right
and allow Love to guide us.

The Keys to the Kingdom
are in the kitchen drawer
with all the stuff
of everyday life.

Playing it safe
is not part of their teaching.
The prophets
and wisdom keepers
call us to a radical witness
of living the sacred truths.

It Might Be a Poem

If you enter deeply
into a prayer,
one that speaks
particularly to you,
saying it often,
writing its words
upon your heart—
the day may come
when you will find
the prayer is praying you.

Lay down the knitting needles of worry
whenever they leap into your hands.
Let anxious thoughts unravel
and peace fill every strand.

Wrap every worry in prayer.
The world may not change,
but you will.
Wrap every worry in prayer.

Before Getting Into Bed

Whoever you are,
whatever your cares
or burdens may be,
lay them down,
turn them over to God to keep.

A symphony of green
shocking in its newness,
so many variations,
Spring.

Yesterday's rain fills a creek
running free
through the city—
sunlight dances on water.

In times of joy or sorrow,
tend the garden
where small blessings grow.

It's Not Complicated

Every day I need
a few poems,
a few prayers,
the voice
of sacred mystery.
Why do I so often forget?

The sound
of one heart
unfolding
after a lifetime
of being
constricted
by fear—
listen.

Seek God
in the wilderness
of your own heart,
in the unspoiled creation
that is within you,
and you will surely find
the Holy One there.

In this time of waiting
and not knowing
how things will unfold,
may you find a pool of calm,
a place of peace and rest
deep within your soul.

It's not about holding
the hands or head
at the right reverential angle
or bending the knees just so.
It's about opening the heart
and taking the risk
of allowing God's love
to touch us and heal us and change us
each day of our lives—
that is the sacred mystery of prayer.

Pray what prayers you can.
Don't stop praying because
there are some words
you cannot say.
The need for prayer
never ends—yours, mine
and millions of others.
Pray what prayers you can.

Meeting for Worship

It is not mine
to judge
another's way
of worship.
I am called,
again and again,
to show up,
to take my seat,
to drop down
into the stillness
where I might hear
God speak to me.

Living With Diminishment

It is a challenge
to accept the truth
of what no longer is possible,
and yet embrace all that still can be.

Tremor as Teacher

Breathless and pushing limits
is a way of life
I can no longer afford to live.
My head and hands have developed
a benign essential tremor
made worse by fatigue and stress,
reminding me to slow down,
breathe deeply and rest.

How difficult it is
to be still,
to surrender
my body, my will,
my everyday life
to the sacred mystery,
the miracle of healing,
and to trust
that this breaking open
and rearranging
of my innermost parts
holds the possibility
of new life
at deeper levels,
not as I would choose
but according to
God's blessing and grace.

I want to read
more good poems
and listen
to less bad news.
Again, and again,
I choose to turn
toward the Light.

O God, help me to see
beyond what is
difficult, discouraging,
depressing,
so that I can feel
your love and light
and experience this day
as a blessing.

Ours is a shape-shifting God,
a shit disturber,
insisting that we take
another look
anytime we refuse
to see the truth
or imagine that we
have things all figured out.
This Holy One invites us
to find the light and love
in the darkest places
and holds us always
in the heart of healing.

Pray me through the hard places,
Lord. I can't do this on my own.
Teach me the way
of yielding to what is needed now,
letting go of my fears
and trusting that you will
pray me through.

You, God, are the infinite source
of the energy essential to all life.
I open my entire being
to receive your love and mercy.
Restore my balance.
Renew my energy.
Fill me with your healing grace.

Practice this:

in this moment,
release
tension and anxiety,

release
fear and sorrow,

release loved ones
to Divine care.

In this moment,
let go,
rest in God,

float in the
light of the Spirit.

Sabbath time—
how hard it is
to trust the truth
that holy rest
restores my soul
and tunes my heart
to God.

Early Spring

Old Redwood Highway
south of Healdsburg,
flowering plum trees
in fullest bloom,
for just a moment
millions
of vibrant pink blossoms
luminous, dazzling,
filled with slanting sun
soon setting light.

Black jewels glistening
in the afternoon light,
thorns that prickle fingers,
a mouthful
of sun-warmed sweetness,
juice running, taste delight—
a blackberry farewell to summer.

Full moon framed
by a luminous corona—
holding back the clouds,
holding me
in a moment of blessing.

A Small Shift Of Awareness

Rearranging my interior furniture
may seem a daunting task,
especially if some of the pieces
are large and hard to move.
Moving a chair or lamp,
opening a window shade,
spending a few moments
with some small treasures
can change
how I see and live this day.

Soul parched days—
only the spring
of eternal waters
can ease my thirst.

Tears surprise me,
welling up
from a wordless place
of ancient sorrow.

To have companions
along the Way,
trusted friends
who see me and love me
as I really am—
this is a healing grace,
a true sharing
of the bread of life.

The pieces of our lives
and all the people
we love
are woven together
only in our hearts—
but oh, what a tapestry!

Persistent bird
watches over sunset waters—
heron lessons
in patience, presence and peace.

Blessing a Birthday

Grow in wisdom, grow in wonder,
walk in beauty—
don't forget your pilgrim feet.
Laugh, love and let go
of all that is not yours to hold.
Sing praises. Dig in the dirt.
Draw boundaries—
paint and dance them, too.
Ride your bike.
Rest in God.
Rejoice!

My body
is sacred space,
home
for the heart of God.

I am asked to live
no life other than my own.
If I will accept
God's grace and guidance,
the path I am to follow
at every turning
will be made known.

I Will Kneel Down

Yielding my body
to the shape of prayer
shifts something
deep within me,
opening
the doors and windows
of my heart
to the healing presence,
power, light and love
of the Eternal One.

This spring,
this new life,
this air
heavy
with hope
stirs in me
green shoots
pushing towards
the light.
This sweetness,
this beauty,
this burning bush
of coral blossoms
calls forth
what cannot
be seen,
and the brilliant
yellow
of the daffodils
echoes in my heart.

Sweet Peas

I plant sweet peas every year
to bring my mother back to me.
For a few weeks in late spring
and early summer,
every time I breathe in
that delicate, sweet smell
and see the sun shine
through those fragile blossoms,
pink, purple, lavender and red,
magenta and two shades of white,
she is here beside me,
cutting sweet peas in the garden
and arranging them
in that effortless way of hers,
so that sweet peas grow in my heart,
and time and distance disappear.

My Granddaughter
Ten Weeks Old

Holding Sophie
while she's sleeping,
what a wordless
hymn of praise—
her heart beating
next to mine,
I feel the Great Love
flowing through us all.

Dahlias

I have fallen in love with dahlias,
the most joyful, exuberant flowers—
hundreds of varieties
in a dazzling array
of knock-your-socks-off colors,
from mignon blooms
less than two inches across,
to twelve-inch giants—
mandalas of the flower world,
fireworks bursting with life.

In a fast-forward world,
I am called to live
a slow-motion life,
tune my heart
to sacred stillness,
find peace, joy
and balance
in the midst of all that is.

For many years
I tried too hard
to understand
the world, my family,
my life.
I sought God
with my mind—
reading, thinking, debating.
I was surprised to find
the doorway
into the world of the Spirit
lies in my heart—
it opened
when I wasn't looking.

Just as tea leaves
steep in hot water,
so do we learn
to live prayerfully.

There is so little I can do—
no words of mine can speak
the truth of your struggle.
May my every breath
become a prayer for you.

Brightly colored padded mittens
designed for kitchen use—
things too hot to handle,
but I will use them
for shadow boxing
and wrestling with God.

Why am I short-tempered
and sharp-tongued
with those I love most?
I need to practice
compassion
and loving kindness
in my own home.

What softens
the hard edges
of my heart
and allows
the tenderness
within me
to be seen?

I need to pray some
of my own poems now,
work with the words
I have been given,
learn from the pages
of my life story
the way of surrender
and of letting go.

Now is the time
to lay down our doubts,
let go of our fears,
claim our strengths,
say what we see,
do what we know,
become fully who
we are meant to be.

Don't Waste a Wish

Whoever you are,
whatever your age,
don't waste a wish.
Take a moment to reflect
and draw a deep breath—
blow out your birthday
candles with care.

Rowing

In the pause
    between strokes of the oars,
in the silence
    that frames speech,
in the place of no thought—
    there I find peace.

In This Moment

What tunes my heart
to the Great Love,
what opens my spirit
to the Light?

Even this gray day
is beautiful.

The sky beginning
to brighten
at the horizon
changes the soft shapes
of nearby islands
and distant mountains.

A light breeze
ripples the water
in shifting patterns
threaded with silver light.

Risk the Light

Pilgrim feet
to the healing path,
drink deeply
at the sacred waters.
Let go of all
that does not belong
to this day
or to this life.
Slow down
to soul time
and listen
to the music
of this earth.
Hold love
with an open hand—
risk the Light.

Tidepool Lessons from the Barnacles

No matter how things look,
or how many times we lose our way,
there is a holiness
that undergirds all of creation
and links us each to each.
Now, so much depends upon
our human willingness
to look for that holiness everywhere
and to call it forth in each other.

Embody peace—
become a witness
to the word.
Let it flow
from the core
of your being
out into the world.
Let every muscle,
bone, fiber, cell
speak
of the deeper truths.
Become
a prayer for peace.

Index of Titles or First Lines

Photographs

Permissions

Several poems were published in *Friendly Woman*: "My body is sacred space" in Vol. 14, #2; "There is a God-space between us," "You, God, are the infinite source," and "It Might Be A Poem" in Vol. 15, #6.

"Risk the Light", "There is a God-space", "Pray me through the hard places", and "Gathering together with the Spirit", have been published in the Redwood Forest Friends Meeting Newsletter.

"Risk the Light" and "With prayers for stillness" were published in the The Vessel, the newsletter of St. David's Episcopal Church in Friday Harbor, WA.

A number of the poems in *A Small Steadying Sail Of Love* were included in *Poems and Prayers*, by Nancy Gibbs Richard, Bellerose Publications, 1991 or *Risk the Light*, a chapbook by Nancy Gibbs Richard, 1998.

Acknowledgments

My father, Zack Gibbs, shared his love of photography with me and gave me my first camera, a Kodak Brownie, when I was in second grade. My mother, Elizabeth Martin Gibbs, shared her love of poetry and writing with me. I grew up in a home where reading books was a part of everyday life. John Manley, high school English teacher at Polytechnic School, introduced me to two poems that changed the direction of my life: Wilfred Owen's "Dulce Et Decorum Est" and Henry Reed's "Naming of Parts". My years of studying French with Renée Geary, also at Poly, and Leonard Pronko, at Pomona College, gave me the gift of reading poetry in a language other than my own. When I was seventeen, R.H. Blyth's four-volume study of Japanese *Haiku* opened my life to spare, meditative verse.

I am grateful to my family and friends, who have encouraged me to take my writing and photography seriously, and who have graciously received small packets of poems and photographs from me over many years.

Two women have midwifed this book into being: Donna Hardy, longtime mentor and friend, editor and co-founder of Angela Center Press; and Deborah Ogden, persistent encourager and friend of many years. I want to thank those whose help has been essential to the making of *A Small Steadying Sail of Love*: Christine van Swearingen, longtime friend, director of the Angela Center and co-founder of Angela Center Press; Bruce

Conway of Illumina Book Design, who has designed
the book with such care; my husband, Charles Richard,
who reads many of my first drafts and often tells me to
grab my camera when he sees a photograph waiting to be
taken; Lynn Trombetta, gifted poet and poetry workshop
leader; the Sonoma County Monday Morning Poets'
Group; Norma Fried, Donna Varnau, Clare Morris, Adam
Graves, Sarah Graves, Donna Richard, Zack Richard,
Jane Mackay, Linda Campbell, Barbara Towner, Nancy
Tiederman, David Bentley, Kathy Littman, Polly Post,
Jane Mills, Elspeth Benton, Brynne Evans, Denise Maas,
Michael Maas, Margaret Forbes and Judith Carter.

My two worshipping communities are part of the
fabric of this book: Redwood Forest Friends Meeting
in Santa Rosa, California, where I have been a member
for twenty years; and Saint David's Episcopal Church in
Friday Harbor, Washington, where my husband Charles
and I attend during the summer months.

For twenty-six years, Angela Center has been a place
of renewal, healing and learning for me, a place where
my spiritual life and my work as a poet and photographer
have been nurtured. I am thankful for all of the staff who
keep the doors to this sacred space open and welcoming
to so many people.

To all those with whom I share prayers and this
journey through life, my deep gratitude.